Mueller Report Graphic Novel

Volume 1

by

Barbara Slate

HUDSON, NY
RICHARD MINSKY
2019

Vol. 1 ISBN: 978-0-937258-09-5
Vol. 2 ISBN: 978-0-937258-10-1

First Edition

This graphic novel is based on the *Report on the Investigation into Russian Interference in the 2016 Presidential Election*, the official report documenting the findings and conclusions of Special Counsel Robert Mueller's investigation into Russian efforts to interfere in the 2016 United States presidential election, allegations of conspiracy or coordination between Donald Trump's presidential campaign and Russia, and allegations of obstruction of justice. A redacted version of the 448-page report was publicly released by the Department of Justice on April 18, 2019. It is divided into two volumes. This edition of *Mueller Report Graphic Novel* interprets and condenses the redacted report and is also issued in two volumes. This is volume 1.

It began with a post...

Jennifer Taub ✔
April 18 · 🌐

Just had a copy made and bound for easier reading.

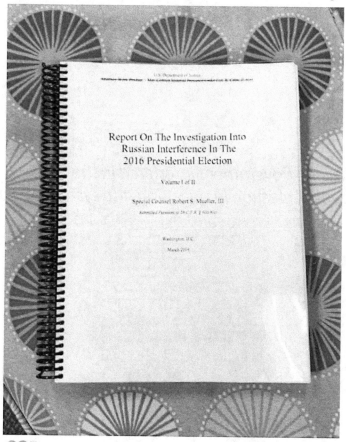

Report On The Investigation Into
Russian Interference In The
2016 Presidential Election

Volume I of II

Special Counsel Robert S. Mueller, III

Washington, D.C.

March 2019

👍❤️😮 401

Barbara Slate Maybe I'll do a graphic novel about it!
Like · Reply

Jennifer Taub ✔ Barbara Slate
🩶 I can't wait til you create this

*The Russian government interfered in the 2016
presidential election in sweeping and systematic fashion.*

Robert S. Mueller, III

THE VOLUNTEER

The Internet Research Agency (IRA) carried out the earliest Russian interference operations— a social media campaign designed to provoke and amplify political and social discord in the United States. The IRA received funding from Russian oligarch Yevgeniy Prigozhin. Prigozhin is widely reported to have ties to Russian President Vladimir Putin.

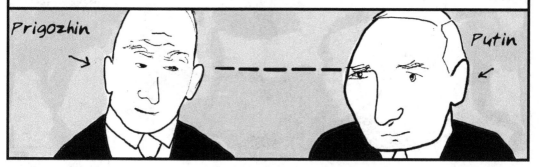

The IRA used social media accounts and interest groups to cause chaos through "information warfare." The campaign was to undermine the U.S. electoral system, a targeted operation that favored candidate Trump and disparaged candidate Clinton.

IRA staged political rallies inside the United States. To organize those rallies, IRA employees posed as U.S. grassroots entities and people, contacting Trump supporters and Campaign officials in the United States.

June 4, 2014, four IRA employees applied to the U.S. Department of State to enter the United States. They lied about their mission, claiming to be four friends who had met at a party. Anna Bogacheva and Aleksandra Krylova received visas and entered the United States. The IRA referred to these employees as "specialists."

The GRU (Main Intelligence Directorate of the General Staff of the Russian Army) began hacking the email accounts of the Clinton Campaign. They stole hundreds of thousands of documents and disseminated the materials through fictitious online personas. The GRU later released additional materials through...

WIKILEAKS

IRA Facebook Groups popped up everywhere with names such as:

Being Patriotic
Stop all Immigrants
Secured Borders
Tea Party News
Black Matters
Blacktivist
Don't Shoot Us
LGBTQ United
United Muslims of America

A Facebook representative testified that Facebook had identified 140 IRA-controlled Facebook accounts that made 80,000 posts and reached 126 million people.

With one click, you could get a "Specialist" friend.

HOW TO ORGANIZE A RALLY IN 6 EASY STEPS

1. Get an IRA specialist to pose as a U.S. grassroots activist.

2. Use a social media persona to promote the rally.

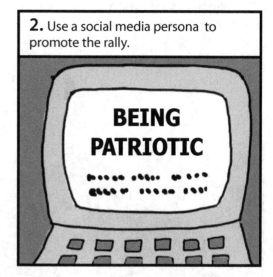

3. Send direct messages to followers.

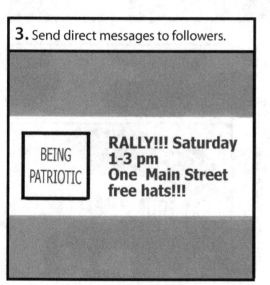

4. Get an enthused U.S. citizen follower to become an event coordinator.

5. Promote the rally by contacting U.S. media with the event coordinator.

6. Post videos and photographs and distribute to IRA vast social media.

Collectively, the IRA's social media accounts reached tens of millions of U.S. citizens. The IRA recruited unsuspecting citizens and criticized Clinton's record as Secretary of State. When the Clinton posts slowed down, a representative was there to remind the specialists...

It is imperative to intensify criticizing Hillary!

How about she's an alien?

Naw. We did that one already.

On Sept 19, 2017 President Trump's personal account @realDonaldTrump responded to a tweet from an IRA-controlled account...

TRUMP RALLY
12-2
30 Green Street
Free hats!

Seconds later...

LOOK!
Mr. Trump posted about our event!

This is great!

The IRA also recruited individuals to perform political acts such as walking around New York City dressed up as Santa Claus with a Trump mask.

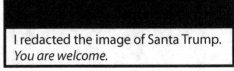

I redacted the image of Santa Trump. *You are welcome.*

THE HILLARY GAME

Whoever destroys her first wins. There are no rules.

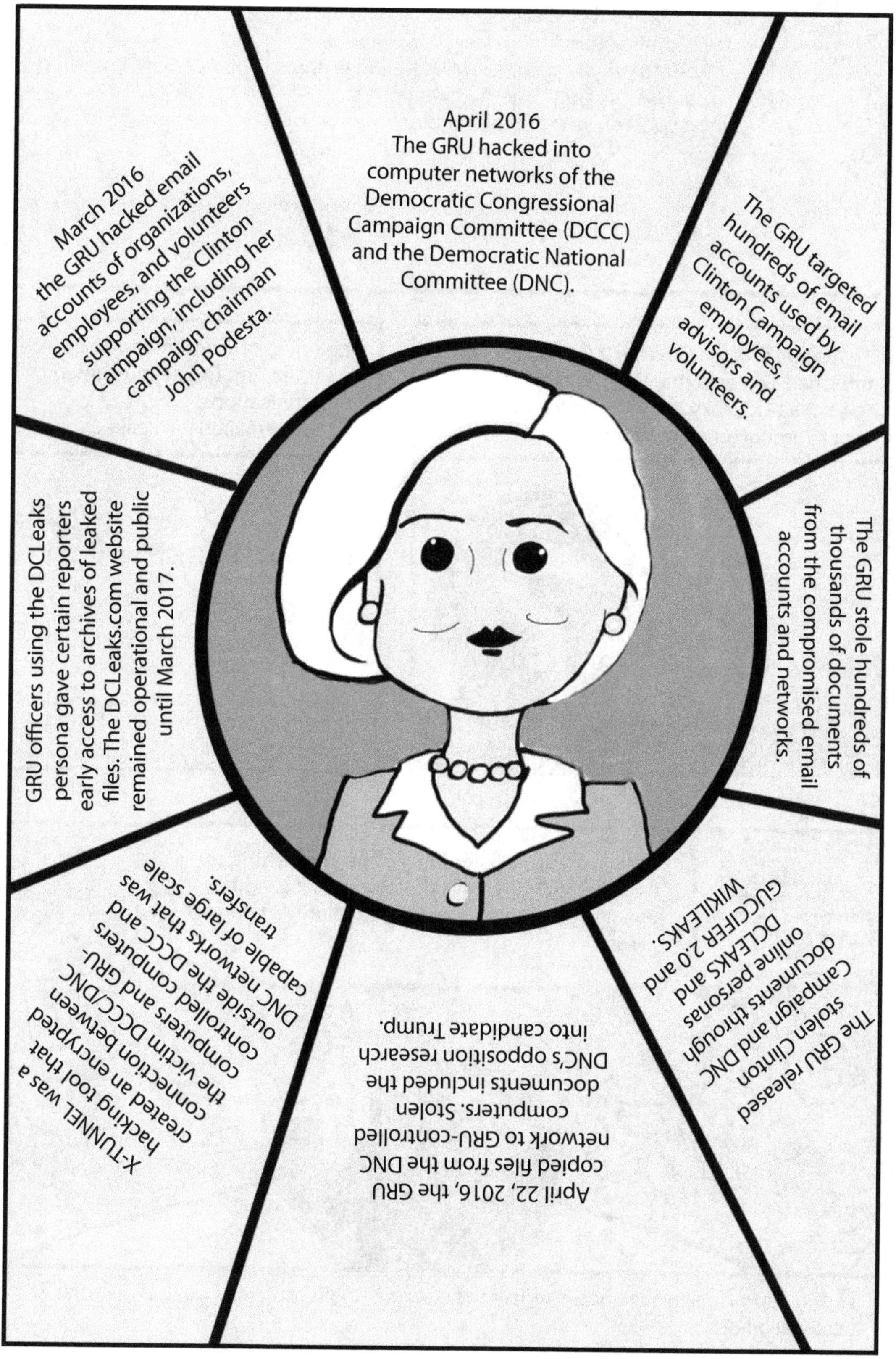
March 2016 the GRU hacked email accounts of organizations, employees, and volunteers supporting the Clinton Campaign, including her campaign chairman John Podesta.
April 2016
The GRU hacked into computer networks of the Democratic Congressional Campaign Committee (DCCC) and the Democratic National Committee (DNC).
The GRU targeted hundreds of email accounts used by Clinton Campaign employees, advisors and volunteers.
The GRU stole hundreds of thousands of documents from the compromised email accounts and networks.
The GRU released stolen Clinton Campaign and DNC documents through online personas DCLEAKS and GUCCIFER 2.0 and WIKILEAKS.
April 22, 2016, the GRU copied files from the DNC network to GRU-controlled computers. Stolen documents included the DNC's opposition research into candidate Trump.
X-TUNNEL was a hacking tool that created an encrypted connection between the victim DCCC/DNC computers and GRU-controlled computers outside the DCCC and DNC networks that was capable of large scale transfers.
GRU officers using the DCLeaks persona gave certain reporters early access to archives of leaked files. The DCLeaks.com website remained operational and public until March 2017.

WIKILEAKS

Communications occurred between WikiLeaks and the GRU-operated persona DCLeaks. On September 15, 2016, @dcleaks wrote to @WikiLeaks ...

> hi there! I'm from DC Leaks. How could we discuss some submission-related issues? Am trying to reach out to you via your secure chat but getting no response. I've got something that might interest you. You won't be disappointed, I promise.

> Hi there.

That same day, the Guccifer 2.0 persona informed DCLeaks that WikiLeaks was trying to contact DCLeaks and arrange for a way to speak through encrypted emails.

Beginning on September 20, 2016, WikiLeaks and DCLeaks resumed communications. DCLeaks emailed Wikileaks ...

> Hi from DCLeaks

The email contained a *PGP-encrypted message.

*Pretty Good Privacy

And soon...

Russia, if you're listening, I hope you're able to find the 30,000 emails that are missing. I think you will probably be rewarded mightily by our press.

Within approximately five hours of Trump's statement, GRU officers targeted Clinton's personal office.

The Trump Campaign showed interest in WikiLeak's releases of hacked materials throughout the summer and fall of 2016.

Harm to Ongoing Matter

In debriefings with the Office*, former deputy campaign chairman Rick Gates said that,

Harm to Ongoing Matter

Harm to Ongoing Matter

Gates recalled candidate
Trump being generally frustrated that the Clinton emails had not been found.

Paul Manafort, who would later become campaign chairman,

Harm to Ongoing Matter

Michael Cohen, former executive vice president of the Trump Organization and special counsel to Donald J. Trump, told the Office that he recalled an incident in which he was in candidate Trump's office in Trump Tower **Harm to Ongoing Matter**

Harm to Ongoing Matter

Cohen further told the Office that, after WikiLeak's subsequent release of stolen DNC emails in July 2016, candidate Trump said to Cohen something to the effect of,

According to Gates, by the late summer of 2016, the Trump Campaign was planning a press strategy, a communications campaign, and messaging based on the possible release of Clinton emails by WikiLeaks. **Harm to Ongoing Matter**

Harm to Ongoing Matter

while Trump and Gates were driving to LaGuardia Airport,
Harm to Ongoing Matter Shortly after
the call candidate Trump told Gates that more releases of damaging information would be coming.

*Office of Special Counsel

On October 7, 2016, the Washington Post published an Access Hollywood video that captured comments by candidate Trump some years earlier. The tape was expected to adversely affect the campaign..

Less than an hour after the video's publication, WikiLeaks released the first set of emails stolen by the Russian Government from the account of Clinton Campaign Chairman John Podesta.

On October 3rd, 2016, Wikileaks sent a twitter direct message to Donald Trump Junior

A PAC run anti-Trump site is about to launch. It is focused on Trump's "unprecedented and dangerous" ties to Russia. We have guessed the password...putintrump

Trump Junior emailed a variety of senior campaign staff...

Guys I got a weird Twitter DM from wikileaks. See below. I tried the password and it works. Not sure if this is anything but it seems like it's really wikileaks asking me as I follow them and it is a DM. Do you know the people mentioned and what the conspiracy they are looking for could be?

On October 3rd, 2016, WikiLeaks sent another direct message to Trump Junior ...

You guys, we need help to disseminate a link alleging candidate Clinton advocated using a drone to target Julian Assange, founder and director of WikiLeaks.

I already did.

October 12, 2016...

It was great to see you and your dad talking about our publications. Strongly suggest your dad tweets this link if he mentions us wlsearch.tk. It will help in "digging through" leaked emails. We just released Podesta emails Part 4.

Two days later, Trump Junior tweeted out...

wlsearch.tk

Throughout 2016, the Trump Campaign expressed great interest in Hillary Clinton's private email server. Trump Campaign advisor Michael Caputo learned through a Florida-based Russian business partner that another Florida-based Russian, Henry Oknyansky (aka Henry Greenberg) claimed to have the goods...

Caputo notified Roger Stone, an American political consultant, and connected Stone and Oknyansky.

Oknyansky and Stone set up a May 2016 in-person meeting.

Oknyansky was accompanied to the meeting by Alexei Rasin, a Ukrainian associate involved in Florida real estate.

Smith wrote that there was a "tug-of-war going on within WikiLeaks over its planned releases in the next few days" and that WikiLeaks "will save its best revelations for last, under the theory this allows little time for response prior to the U.S. election November 8."

An attachment to the email claimed that WikiLeaks would release "All 33k deleted Emails" by "November 1st."

No emails obtained from Clinton's server were subsequently released.

Rasin offered to sell Stone derogatory info on Clinton. Stone refused.

Trump asked individuals affiliated with his campaign to find the deleted emails

The SEARCH FOR THE 30,000 MISSING EMAILS

Smith continued to send emails to an undisclosed recipient list about Clinton's deleted emails until shortly before the election.

Michael Flynn, who would later serve as National Security Advisor in the Trump Administration, recalled that he made this request repeatedly.

In early September 2016, Smith circulated a document stating that his initiative was "in coordination" with the Trump Campaign, "to the extent permitted as an independent expenditure organization." The document listed multiple individuals affiliated with the Trump campaign.

A backup of Smith's computer contained two files that had been downloaded from WikiLeaks and were originally attached to emails received by John Podesta.

Flynn contacted Senate staffer Barbara Ledeen (who began her efforts to obtain the emails in December 2015) and Peter Smith, an investment advisor.

December 3, 2015, Ledeen emailed Smith a proposal to obtain the emails and attached a 25-page proposal stating that "The Clinton email server was breached long ago. The Chinese, Russian and Iranian intelligence services could reassemble the server's email content.

Smith made claims that he was in contact with hackers with "ties and affiliations to Russia" who had access to the emails, and that his efforts were coordinated with the Trump campaign.

September 2016, Smith and Ledeen got back in touch. Ledeen claimed to have obtained a trove of emails (from the "dark web") that purported to be the deleted Clinton emails. A tech advisor determined the emails were not authentic.

He created a company, raised tens of thousands of dollars, and recruited security experts and business associates.

Smith tried to locate and obtain the emails himself.

Smith forwarded the proposal to two colleagues. On December 16, 2015, Smith declined to participate in her "initiative."

September 2015, Felix Sater, a N.Y. real estate adviser, contacted Michael Cohen, executive vice president of the Trump Organization...

Buddy, let's do a Trump/Moscow Tower!

Cohen obtained approval from candidate Trump , who was then president of the Trump Organization. Cohen kept Trump up-to-date on the progress of Trump/Moscow...

It's continuing, Boss.

Cohen consulted with Ivanka, first daughter and advisor to the President, about the Trump/Moscow Tower...

I think I'll go with the Corinthian columns.

Trump/Moscow Project

...and Trump Junior, about his possible involvement...

I would be invaluable. I have so much Moscow experience.

On September 22, 2015, Cohen forwarded a preliminary design for Trump Moscow to Rtskhiladze, an executive who had pursued business ventures in Moscow.

Cohen wrote...

I look forward to your reply about this spectacular project in Moscow.

Rtskhiladze replied...

If we could organize the meeting in New York at the highest level of the Russian Government and Mr. Trump this project would definitely receive the worldwide attention.

Later, Rtskhiladze sent another email...

The Trump/Moscow Tower will be a symbol of stronger economic, business and cultural relationships between New York and Moscow and therefore United States and the Russian Federation.

Trump signed an LOI (letter of intent).

The LOI included...

Residential, Hotel, Commercial, and Office components,

250 first class luxury residential condominiums,

one first class luxury hotel consisting of approximately 15 floors and containing not fewer than 150 hotel rooms.

$4 million up front fee prior to ground breaking to the Trump Organization.

TRUMP
MOSCOW

On November 3, 2015, the day after the Trump Organization transmitted the LOI, Felix Sater emailed Cohen ...

Buddy, our boy can become President of the USA and we can engineer it. I will get all of Putins team to buy in on this, I will manage this process. You and I will get Donald and Vladimir on a stage together very shortly.

Michael lets go. 2 boys from Brooklyn getting a USA president elected. This is good really good.

PAPADOPOULOS

In the summer of 2015, George Papadopoulos sought a role as a foreign policy advisor to the Trump campaign but was getting nowhere.

The Trump Campaign is not hiring policy advisors.

Papadopoulos persisted. At the time of a March 2 email, the Trump Campaign was getting criticized for lack of experienced foreign policy advisors.

The best...the smartest.

Who's your foreign team?

What's your policy?

What's your experience?

Later, Trump demanded...

GET ME A FOREIGN POLICY TEAM!

TRUMP

A campaign official gave Papadopoulos's name to Sam Clovis, Trump's chief policy advisor. And soon...

Congratulations! You have a role as a foreign policy advisor to the Trump Campaign.

Russia will be important in the Campaign's foreign policy.

George Papadopoulos is the best and smartest.

Who?

How do you spell that?

Papadopoulos was a foreign policy advisor to the Campaign from March to October 2016.

In late April, Papadopoulos was told by London-based professor Joseph Mifsud that the Russian Government had "dirt" on Clinton in the form of thousands of emails. It could assist the Campaign through the anonymous release of information that would be damaging to candidate Clinton.

These connections could increase my importance as a policy advisor in the Trump administration.

Papadopoulos sent an email to members of the Trump Foreign policy advisory team. The subject line was "Meeting with Russian leadership—including Putin. "

Just finished a very productive lunch with a good friend, Joseph Mifsud, the director of the London Academy of Diplomacy. The topic was to arrange a meeting between us and the Russian leadership. They are keen to host us in a "neutral" city or Moscow. Putin is ready to meet. Waiting for everyone's thoughts.

Clovis responded...

This is most informative. We probably should not go forward until we sit with our NATO allies. We need to reassure them that we are not going to advance anything with Russia until we have everyone on the same page.

More thoughts later today. Great work.

March 31, 2016 meeting of the foreign policy team...

I have learned through my contacts in London that Putin wants to meet with Trump. My connections could help arrange a meeting.

Trump was interested and receptive to the idea of a meeting.

THE TRUMP TOWER MEETING

Donald Trump Junior got an email from Robert Goldstone, a British publicist and music manager, at the request of his client...

...Russian pop star Emin Agalarov.

Emin is the son of Aras Agalarov, a Russian billionaire businessman and property developer with ties to Putin.

Aras worked with Trump in connection with the 2013 Miss Universe pageant in Moscow. He arranged to get Putin a special invitation from Trump to attend the pageant.

Is he here yet?

But Putin was a no show.

Back in NYC, Aras's daughter delivered a special gift for Mr. Trump.

It's from Russia.

It was a black lacquered box. Inside was a sealed letter from Putin.

What the letter said has never been revealed.

The email to Donald Trump Junior from the music manager read...

Good morning,
Emin just called and asked me to contact you with something very interesting.
The Crown prosecutor of Russia offered to provide the Trump Campaign with some official documents and information that would incriminate Hillary and her dealings with Russia and would be very useful to your father. This is very sensitive but is part of Russia and its government support for Trump.
Best,
Rob Goldstone

Minutes later Trump Junior responded...

If it's what you say I love it

Trump Junior and the pop star had multiple conversations. A meeting was in the works.

Trump Junior invited campaign chairman Paul Manafort and Senior advisor Jared Kushner to attend the meeting.

See you there.

Put me down for a 4 o'clock with Junior.

Much of the staff knew about the meeting. Cohen recalls Trump Junior leaning in to tell Trump Senior the news...

The dirt on Hillary meeting is on.

According to written answers submitted by President Trump, he has no recollection of learning about the meeting.

Meeting? What meeting?

June 9, 2016, Trump Tower...

Manafort, Trump Junior, and Jared Kushner met with

Ike Kaveladze, VP of Aras Algarov's company

Natalia Veselnitskaya, a Russian attorney,

Goldstone, the music manager

Samochornov, a translator

Akhmetshin, a Russian lobbyist.

Natalia Veselnitskaya provided dirt...

Funds derived from illegal activities in Russia were provided to Hillary.

Trump Junior wanted to know...

Do you have proof?

I lost track when the money arrived in the U. S.

but while we're on the subject, the Magnitsky Act is unfair! Why impose sanctions on Russia when we have done nothing wrong?!

TRUMP

Kushner sent emails to assistants at Kushner Companies...

Call me. I need an excuse to get out of this meeting.

BRRRRING!!!

What? Okay I'll be right there!

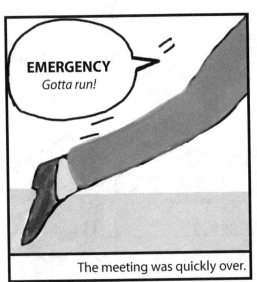

EMERGENCY
Gotta run!

The meeting was quickly over.

The meeting became public in July 2017.

There was a meeting at Trump Tower with at least 3 Russians. Donald Trump Junior, Manafort and Jared Kushner attended.

BREAKING NEWS

Don Junior explained...

It was a nothing burger.

The next month Goldstone commented to Emin about the volume of publicity the June 9 meeting had generated...

Now the FBI is on it. My reputation is destroyed by this dumb meeting.

RUSSIA

Trump wanted to change his 2012 view ...

RUSSIA IS THE NUMBER ONE THREAT TO OUR COUNTRY!

to his 2016 view....

LET'S BE FRIENDS.

During the week of the National Republican Convention (NRC) Trump campaign officials met with Russian Ambassador Sergey Kislyak, a Senior Russian diplomat and politician.

Soon after, J.D. Gordon, a senior advisor on policy and national security to the Trump Campaign, watered down a proposed amendment to the Republican party platform...

I request that "lethal" assistance to Ukraine in response to Russian aggression be changed to "appropriate" assistance.

U.S. arming Ukrainians in the fight against the pro-Russian forces was staunchly opposed by the Russian government.

Diana Denman, a Republican delegate who supported arming U.S. allies in Ukraine reported...

J.D. Gordon told me that Trump directed him to support weakening the position in the platform.

Ultimately, the watered down version was adopted. When asked about the reason Trump was for changing the amendment...

Amendment? What amendment?

March 2016 Donald Trump pronounced to Paul Manafort...

YOU'RE HIRED.

It is an honor, Sir. I'll work for free.

Mar-a-Lago

Paul Manafort served on the Trump Campaign, including as Campaign Chairman, from March to August 2016.

Manafort had connections to Russia through his prior work for Russian oligarch Oleg Vladimirovich Deripaska (OVD) a billionaire tycoon with close ties to Putin...

... and connections through work for a pro-Russian regime in Ukraine.

OVD filed a suit in New York State court claiming Manafort and Rick Gates, Manafort's deputy on the Campaign and longtime assistant, defrauded him of $18.9 million.

NEW YORK STATE COURT

Manafort was concerned...

How am I ever going to pay OVD back?

Manafort devised a plan...

Manafort instructed Gates to provide Kilimnik, a Russian/Ukrainian political consultant and Russian intelligence operative, with updates on the Trump Campaign.

Kilimnik

Manafort expected Kilimnik to share the information with OVD, and with three Ukrainian oligarchs...

Serhiy Lyovochkin

Akhmetov

Boris Kolesnikov

Manafort emailed Kilimnik...

Have you shown "our friends" the media coverage of my new role?

Absolutely. Every article.

How do we use to get whole. Has **OVD** operation seen?

Yes I have been sending everything

April 2016 Manafort instructed Gates to send internal polling data prepared for the Trump campaign, sometimes via WhatsApp...

"internal polling" described the status of the Trump Campaign and Manafort's role in it, and assessed Trump's prospects for victory.

Gates then deleted communications on a daily basis,

DELETE

Manafort emailed Kilimnik ...

Any movement on this issue with our friend?

I am carefully optimistic on the question of our biggest interest.

If he needs private briefings we can accommodate.

Manafort met with Kilimnik to discuss three issues. First, a plan to resolve the political problems in Ukraine. This included a "backdoor" means for Russia to control eastern Ukraine. Kilimnik told Manafort...

All we need is a wink and perhaps a nudge from DT.

Second, Manafort briefed Kilimnik on the state of the Trump campaign.

BATTLEGROUND STATES

Michigan
Wisconsin
Pennsylvania
Minnesota

Third, they discussed two financial matters: the lawsuit, and 2 mil owed to Manafort for consulting work for Ukrainians. Manafort was concerned...

Come on. I've given them millions worth of info. You gotta get OVD to drop this damn lawsuit.

The press started tracking Manafort.

NEWS

MANAFORT SHARED 2016 DATA WITH RUSSIAN PAL

Manafort had to resign from the Trump Campaign.

It's been a pleasure to serve.

TRUMP

Trump acknowledged Manafort's fine work.

I am very appreciative for his great work in helping to get us where we are today, and in particular his work guiding us through the delegate and convention process. Paul is a true professional and I wish him the greatest success.

Although no longer part of the team, Manafort continued to offer advice to campaign officials.

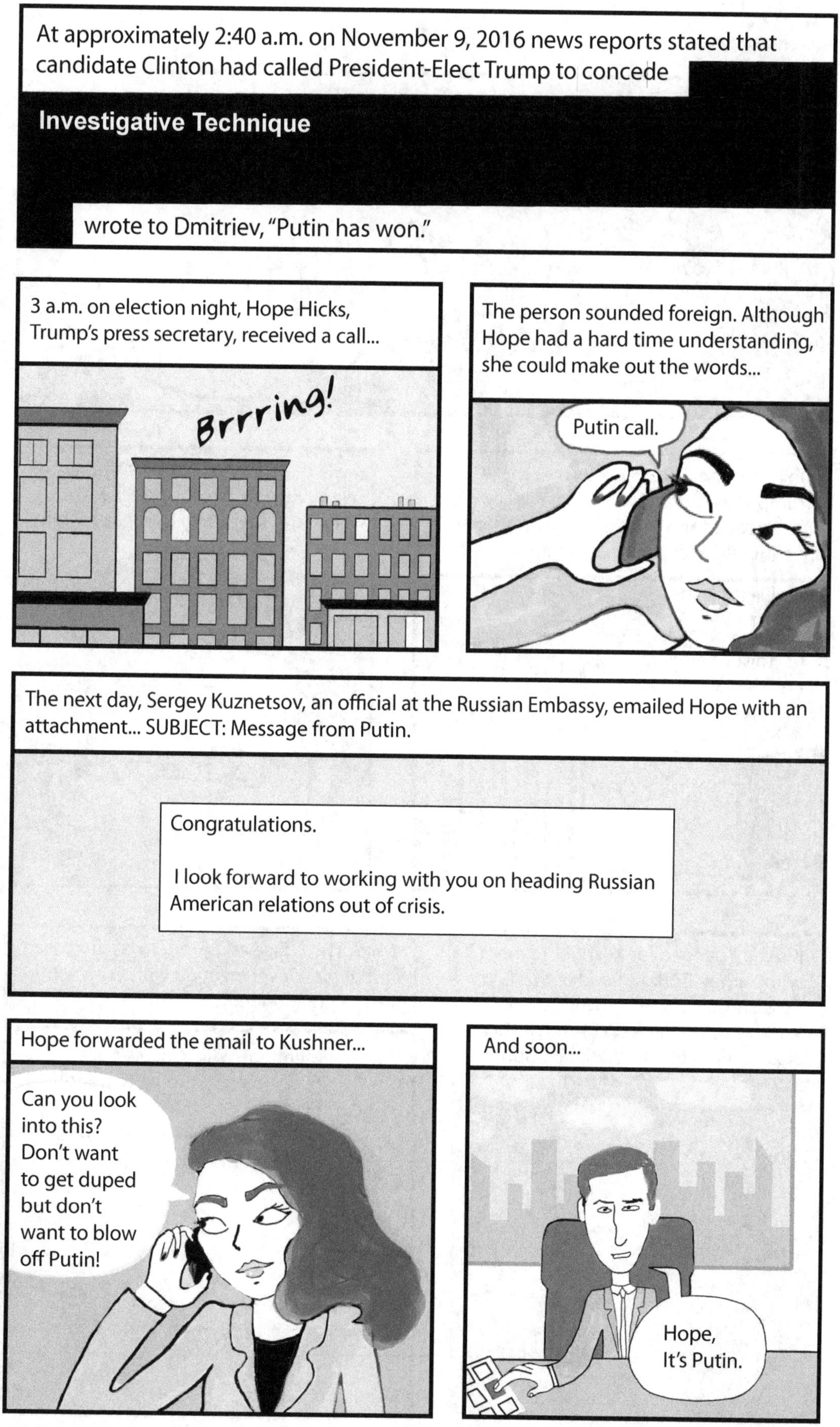
At approximately 2:40 a.m. on November 9, 2016 news reports stated that candidate Clinton had called President-Elect Trump to concede [redacted]
Investigative Technique
[redacted] wrote to Dmitriev, "Putin has won."
3 a.m. on election night, Hope Hicks, Trump's press secretary, received a call...
Brrring!
The person sounded foreign. Although Hope had a hard time understanding, she could make out the words...
Putin call.
The next day, Sergey Kuznetsov, an official at the Russian Embassy, emailed Hope with an attachment... SUBJECT: Message from Putin.
Congratulations.
I look forward to working with you on heading Russian American relations out of crisis.
Hope forwarded the email to Kushner...
Can you look into this? Don't want to get duped but don't want to blow off Putin!
And soon...
Hope, It's Putin.

Five days later, Trump and Putin spoke by phone.

On November 30, 2016, Kushner met at Trump Tower with Kislyak, the Russian Ambassador and Michael Flynn, National Security Advisor. Kushner began...

We would like to start afresh with U.S. Russian relations...

I will need someone to communicate with who has direct contact with Putin and the ability to speak for him.

Kislyak arranged for Kushner to meet with Sergey Gorkov, head of the Russian-government-owned bank Vnesheconombank (VEB) with a very close connection to Vladimir Putin.

When The Office asked what was discussed at that high level meeting with Gorkov, Kushner responded...

Meeting? With Gorkov? We never even bothered to google his name.

Two months before the election...

U.S. intelligence officials concluded that Putin was directly involved in his government's efforts to meddle in the election. Sept. 5, 2016, then President Barack Obama warned Putin...

Cut it out.

The warning went unheeded. After the election, President Obama signed an Executive Order imposing many sanctions on Russia:

Imposed sanctions on nine Russian individuals and entities.

Expelled 35 Russian government officials.

Closed two Russian government-owned compounds in the U.S.

In a meeting at Mar-a-Lago, senior officials and President Elect Trump were concerned that these sanctions would harm U.S. relations with Russia.

And we were just starting to bond.

Obama spoils everything.

Mar-a-Lago

The Press wanted to know...

Are you imposing sanctions on Russia?

I think we ought to get on with our lives.

Incoming National Security Advisor Michael Flynn was the Transition Team's primary conduit for communications with Russian Ambassador Kislyak.

Flynn was anxiously waiting to hear from the Mar-a-Lago team as to how to handle the sanctions. Flynn got word...

Make sure the situation does not get out of hand.

Flynn called Kislyak...

Don't do a tit for tat.

Soon Putin released a statement...

Russia will not take retaliatory measures in response to the sanctions at this time.

Trump tweeted...

Donald J. Trump

Great move on delay (by V. Putin).
I always knew he was smart.

At a briefing, Trump asked K.T. McFarland, Flynn's incoming deputy...

Was it the Russians?

Yes.

It could be the Russians or it could also be somebody sitting on their bed that weighs 400 pounds.

On July 13, 2018, a federal grand jury returned an indictment charging Russian military intelligence officers with conspiring to hack into U.S. computers used by the Clinton Campaign, DNC, DCCC, steal documents from those computers, and stage releases of the stolen documents to interfere in the election. The indictment also describes how, in staging the releases, the defendants used the Guccifer 2.0 persona to disseminate documents through WikiLeaks; and a separate conspiracy to hack into the computers of U.S. persons and entities responsible for the administration of the 2016 U.S. election.

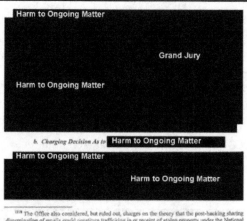

Harm to Ongoing Matter

Grand Jury

Harm to Ongoing Matter

b. *Charging Decision As to* Harm to Ongoing Matter

Harm to Ongoing Matter

Harm to Ongoing Matter

[1318] The Office also considered, but ruled out, charges on the theory that the post-hacking sharing dissemination of emails could constitute trafficking in or receipt of stolen property under the National len Property Act (NSPA), 18 U.S.C. §§ 2314 and 2315. The statutes comprising the NSPA cover ods, wares, or merchandise," and lower courts have largely understood that phrase to be limited to gible items since the Supreme Court's decision in *Dowling v. United States*, 473 U.S. 207 (1985). *See ted States v. Yijia Zhang*, 995 F. Supp. 2d 340, 344-48 (E.D. Pa. 2014) (collecting cases). One of those t-*Dowling* decisions—*United States v. Brown*, 925 F.2d 1301 (10th Cir. 1991)—specifically held that NSPA does not reach "a computer program in source code form," even though that code was stored in gible items (*i.e.*, a hard disk and in a three-ring notebook). *Id.* at 1302-03. Congress, in turn, cited the wn opinion in explaining the need for amendments to 18 U.S.C. § 1030(a)(2) that "would ensure that theft of intangible information by the unauthorized use of a computer is prohibited in the same way theft physical items [is] protected." S. Rep. 104-357, at 7 (1996). That sequence of events would make it cult to argue that hacked emails in electronic form, which are the relevant stolen items here, constitute ods, wares, or merchandise" within the meaning of the NSPA.

176

Harm to Ongoing Matter

Harm to Ongoing Matter

Harm to Ongoing Matter

177

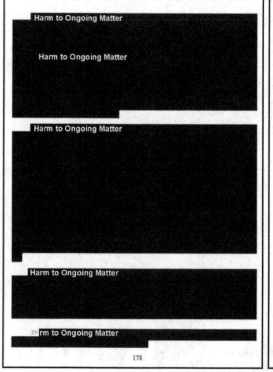

Harm to Ongoing Matter

Harm to Ongoing Matter

Harm to Ongoing Matter

Harm to Ongoing Matter

:rm to Ongoing Matter

178

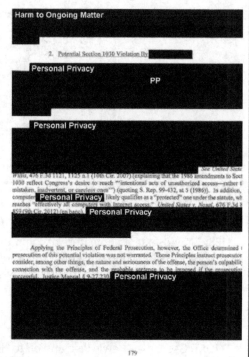

Harm to Ongoing Matter

2. Potential Section 1030 Violation By

Personal Privacy

PP

Personal Privacy

See United State Willis, 476 F.3d 1121, 1125 n.1 (10th Cir. 2007) (explaining that the 1986 amendments to Sect 1030 reflect Congress's desire to reach "'intentional acts of unauthorized access—rather t mistaken, inadvertent, or careless ones'") (quoting S. Rep. 99-432, at 5 (1986)). In addition, computer Personal Privacy likely qualifies as a "protected" one under the statute, wh reaches "effectively all computers with Internet access." *United States v. Nosal*, 676 F.3d 8 859 (9th Cir. 2012) (en banc). Personal Privacy

Applying the Principles of Federal Prosecution, however, the Office determined prosecution of this potential violation was not warranted. Those Principles instruct prosecutor consider, among other things, the nature and seriousness of the offense, the person's culpabilit connection with the offense, and the probable sentence to be imposed if the prosecutio successful. Justice Manual § 9-27.230 Personal Privacy

179

Although the evidence of contacts between Trump Campaign officials and Russia-affiliated individuals may not have been sufficient to establish or sustain criminal charges, several U.S. persons connected to the campaign made false statements about those contacts and took other steps to obstruct the Office's investigation and those of Congress. The office therefore charged some of those individuals with making false statements and obstructing justice.

NAME: Paul Manafort

TITLE: Campaign Chairman for Trump Campaign

CONSPIRACY: (1) to defraud the United States and to commit offenses against the United States, and (2) to obstruct justice (witness tampering).

SENTENCE: 73 months

NAME: Rick Gates

TITLE: Manafort deputy

CONSPIRACY: to defraud and commit multiple offenses against the United States, and making false statements to the Office.

PLEA: Guilty—struck a deal

NAME: Michael Flynn

TITLE: National Security Advisor to the President

LIE: Content of conversations with Kislyak when U.S. had imposed sanctions on Russia.

PLEA: Guilty to making false statements

SENTENCE: Waiting

NAME: Michael Cohen

TITLE: Executive Vice-president and special counsel to the Trump Organization

LIE: when the Trump Moscow project ended, to minimize the links between the project and Trump (who by this time was president).

SENTENCE: 3 years

NAME: George Papadopoulos

TITLE: Foreign Policy advisor to the Trump Campaign

LIES: Timing, extent and nature of communications with the Russians, lying that communications occurred before joining the Trump Campaign.

PLEA: Guilty to making false statements to the FBI.

SENTENCE: 14 days in prison, $9,500 fine , 200 hours of community service.

TODAY: George is a newly wed and off to Hollywood.

If we had had confidence that the president clearly did not commit a crime, we would have said so.

Russian intelligence officers, who are part of the Russian military, launched a concerted attack on our political system.

Charging the president with a crime was not an option we could consider. You cannot charge a sitting president. It is unconstitutional.

And I will close by reiterating the central allegation of our indictments, that there were multiple, systematic efforts to interfere in our election.

And that allegation deserves the attention of every American. Thank you. Thank you for being here today.

CPSIA information can be obtained
at www.ICGtesting.com
Printed in the USA
BVHW010231260619
551925BV00001BA/2/P

9 780937 258095